WOMEN LEADING THE WAY

Vera Wang

Fashion Designer

by Kate Moening

BELLWETHER MEDIA • MINNEAPOLIS, MN

Note to Librarians, Teachers, and Parents:

Blastoff! Readers are carefully developed by literacy experts and combine standards-based content with developmentally appropriate text.

Level 1 provides the most support through repetition of high-frequency words, light text, predictable sentence patterns, and strong visual support.

Level 2 offers early readers a bit more challenge through varied simple sentences, increased text load, and less repetition of high-frequency words.

Level 3 advances early-fluent readers toward fluency through increased text and concept load, less reliance on visuals, longer sentences, and more literary language.

Level 4 builds reading stamina by providing more text per page, increased use of punctuation, greater variation in sentence patterns, and increasingly challenging vocabulary.

Level 5 encourages children to move from "learning to read" to "reading to learn" by providing even more text, varied writing styles, and less familiar topics.

Whichever book is right for your reader, Blastoff! Readers are the perfect books to build confidence and encourage a love of reading that will last a lifetime!

This edition first published in 2020 by Bellwether Media, Inc.

No part of this publication may be reproduced in whole or in part without written permission of the publisher. For information regarding permission, write to Bellwether Media, Inc., Attention: Permissions Department, 6012 Blue Circle Drive, Minnetonka, MN 55343.

Library of Congress Cataloging-in-Publication Data

Names: Moening, Kate, author.
Title: Vera Wang : fashion designer / Kate Moening.
Other titles: Blastoff! readers. 2, Women leading the way.
Description: Minneapolis, MN : Bellwether Media, 2020. | Series: Blastoff! readers. Women leading the way | Includes bibliographical references and index. | Audience: Ages 5-8 | Audience: Grades K-1 | Summary: "Relevant images match informative text in this introduction to Vera Wang. Intended for students in kindergarten through third grade"–Provided by publisher" Identifiers: LCCN 2019024655 (print) | LCCN 2019024656 (ebook) | ISBN 9781644871249 (library binding) | ISBN 9781618918000 (paperback) | ISBN 9781618917805 (ebook)
Subjects: LCSH: Wang, Vera–Juvenile literature. | Women fashion designers–Biography–Juvenile literature. Fashion designers–Biography–Juvenile literature.
Classification: LCC TT505.W36 M64 2020 (print) | LCC TT505.W36 (ebook) | DDC 746.9/2092 [B]–dc23
LC record available at https://lccn.loc.gov/2019024655
LC ebook record available at https://lccn.loc.gov/2019024656

Editor: Al Albertson   Designer: Andrea Schneider

Printed in the United States of America, North Mankato, MN.

Table of Contents

Who Is Vera Wang?

Vera Wang is a **fashion designer**. People all over the world love her clothes and **accessories**!

Vera is especially known for her beautiful wedding dresses.

"I WAS FEARLESS BECAUSE I REALLY DIDN'T KNOW ANY BETTER." (2013)

Vera grew up in New York City.
She loved to ice skate!

people ice skating in
New York City

ROCK CENTER CAFÉ

New York

New York City

N
W
E
S

She hoped to skate in the **Olympics**.

Getting Her Start

Vera at the Vera Wang
Collection Show in 2014

Vera did not make the
Olympic team. She decided
to work in fashion instead.

After college, Vera worked at a famous fashion magazine called *Vogue*.

Vera Wang Profile

Birthday: June 27, 1949

Hometown: New York City, New York

Field: fashion design

Schooling: studied art history

Influences:
- **Frances Patiky Stein** (***Vogue*** **fashion director**)
- **Polly Allen Mellen (fashion editor)**

Vera worked hard at *Vogue*. She learned as much as she could.

But Vera wanted to do more than write about clothes. She dreamed of designing them!

Vera with *Vogue* editor Anna Wintour

Changing the World

Vera's designs from 1990

In 1989, Vera took a chance on her dream. She designed her own wedding dress!

She soon opened her first dress shop. People loved Vera's work!

Vera at a store opening in 2010

13

Running a fashion **company** was hard. It was not easy to think of bold new ideas every **season**.

But Vera trusted herself. She kept working!

Vera at her runway
show in 2004

Vera's dresses became known for their **unique** colors and **details**.

Vera made other clothes, too. She even made outfits for Olympic ice skaters!

Olympic medalist Michelle Kwan in Vera Wang design

Today, Vera still runs her company.

Vera Wang Timeline

1972   Vera becomes the youngest editor to work at *Vogue* magazine

1990   Vera opens her first store in New York City

2005   Vera is named Womenswear Designer of the Year by the Council of Fashion Designers of America (CFDA)

2012   Vera opens a store in Seoul, South Korea, her first store in Asia

2013   Vera wins the Geoffrey Beene Lifetime Achievement Award from the CFDA

She has opened clothing stores in Asia, Europe, and Australia!

Many famous people have worn Vera's dresses. She has taught people to see clothing in new ways.

She **inspires** artists around the world to move fashion forward!

Michelle Obama in a Vera Wang dress

"SUCCESS SHOULD BE **DEFINED ON YOUR OWN TERMS.**" (2013)

Glossary

accessories—objects such as jewelry or shoes that add to the look of an outfit

company—a group that makes, buys, or sells goods for money

details—certain small parts of something

fashion designer—a person who plans and makes new clothing, accessories, or footwear

inspires—gives someone an idea about what to do or create

Olympics—short for Olympic Games; the Olympic Games are worldwide summer or winter sports contests held in a different country every four years.

season—a period of time during the year when fashion designers show their latest designs

unique—different or new

To Learn More

AT THE LIBRARY
Balzekas, Leigh Anne, and Kristine Ownley. *Fashion Design*. Vero Beach, Fla.: Rourke Education Media, 2019.

Higgins, Nadia. *Clothing Then and Now*. Minneapolis, Minn.: Jump!, 2019.

Leaf, Christina. *Zaha Hadid: Architect*. Minneapolis, Minn.: Bellwether Media, 2019.

ON THE WEB

FACTSURFER

Factsurfer.com gives you a safe, fun way to find more information.

1. Go to www.factsurfer.com.

2. Enter "Vera Wang" into the search box and click 🔍.

3. Select your book cover to see a list of related web sites.

Index